The Official Real Estate Investors Guide to LEGALLY Minimizing Your Taxes

Larry M. Weinstein, CPA

Certified Tax Reduction Strategist™
Director of National Tax Practice
www.TaxSavingsForRealEstateInvestors.com

9639 Hillcroft, Suite 820
Houston, Texas 77096
(713) 726-1603 voice
(832) 202-2500 fax

Larry@Weinstein-CPA.com

This book presents information that is factual as of the time of publication. The information presented here is of a general nature.

How the IRS rules and regulations should best be applied is different in every taxpayer's unique case. Accordingly, no liability can be assumed in how the information is applied to your particular personal situation.

No client relationship has been
created or can be inferred by purchase of this book.

Table of Contents

Why I Wrote This Book

There are many tax strategies that can be implemented by a Real Estate Investor to help reduce the amount of taxes they must pay.

There seems to be much information floating around in the media and on the Internet, but it is all in "bits and pieces."

Clients who become Real Estate Investors commonly ask, "Should I incorporate?" or "Should I form an LLC?" Can I deduct this expense or that expense?

I have not yet found a single source of information that describes all the strategies that can be used by a Real Estate Investor to minimize their taxes.

For this reason I have taken the time to pull all of the guidelines and information together in a logical framework in one place, to assist Real Estate Investors in evaluating all of their options.

Also included in this book, is a summarization of all of the entities from which an Investor has to choose, providing a description of what they are, how they work, their significant tax and non-tax considerations, the advantages and disadvantages of each entity, who the entity is best suited for, and those for whom the entity is not the best option.

I hope that you find the answers you are looking for in this book.

Introduction

There are many things to consider when you become a Real Estate Investor.

Over your lifetime, taxes are the single largest expenditure that a taxpayer makes. Much more than their mortgage or even their cars.

The Tax Foundation, a Washington, D.C., tax research organization, calculates that Tax Freedom Day®, the day of the year in which taxpayers have earned enough to pay all of their tax obligations, was April 24th for 2016.

Americans collectively spent more on taxes in 2016 than they did for food, clothing, and housing combined.

One of the biggest challenges you'll face on a regular basis is how to minimize the taxes that you pay.

As a Real Estate Investor, you have the opportunity to implement various tax strategies to help you reduce the taxes that you pay.

Some of these options can literally save you thousands of tax dollars.

And many of these options are unavailable to taxpayers who have a job and are employees, rather than being their own boss.

However, you must take positive, proactive steps to structure your affairs to legally pay the least amount of tax as possible.

Sharing some of the commonly used tax reduction strategies for Real Estate Investors is the sole focus of this book.

Selecting and implementing the appropriate tax strategies will have a direct impact on how you operate as a Real Estate Investor, what benefits you will personally receive, how much you will ultimately pay in tax and how you will accumulate wealth.

Chapter 1

Real Estate Investors Beware

"In this world nothing is certain but death and taxes."
Benjamin Franklin

The IRS wants to get into your wallets. Real estate is still one of the most tax advantageous investments you can own. Real estate can make you very wealthy if you know how to apply the tax laws to your advantage. How do I know this?

For over 30 years, I have been a tax advisor to the real estate industry.

During my career, I have represented, counseled, and done high level strategic tax planning and preparation for scores of real estate clients ranging from brand new investors to a multi-millionaire real estate investor with over 25 apartment complexes, and everything in between.

I am also a real estate investor and landlord myself. My over 30 years of experience tells me that most real estate investors are overpaying their taxes and, most likely, you are overpaying your taxes as well!!

I have spent hundreds of hours researching the tax laws that apply to residential and commercial real estate investors.

Based on my research and experience, I have discovered 16 strategies that, if properly implemented, will LEGALLY minimize the amount of taxes you pay each , more quickly build your wealth every year and put more cash in your pocket.

"The income tax has made more liars
out of the American people than golf has.
Will Rogers

Chapter 2
What is Tax Planning?

"Anyone may arrange his affairs so that his taxes shall be as low as possible; he is not bound to choose that pattern which best pays the treasury. There is not even a patriotic duty to increase one's taxes. Over and over again the Courts have said that there is nothing sinister in so arranging affairs as to keep taxes as low as possible. Everyone does it, rich and poor alike and all do right, for nobody owes a public duty to pay more than the law demands."
Judge Learned Hand, 1935

Tax planning is the process of evaluating the various options and strategies available, to determine when, whether, and how to conduct both business and personal transactions to either reduce or eliminate taxes.

Courts have upheld your right to structure your affairs in a manner that ***legally*** lowers your tax liability. Known as tax planning or ***tax avoidance***, this is completely legal.

Tax evasion, however, is the reduction of tax through illegal, fraudulent means. What distinguishes tax avoidance from tax evasion generally is a result of fraud.

Tax evasion occurs when you have already incurred a tax but attempt to change the facts, to avoid the resulting tax implications.

Some of the main areas in which taxpayers commit fraud include but are not limited to:

- Accounting irregularities, including failure to keep adequate books and records, or reporting less income on one's tax returns than have been reported in the accounting records.
- Understating income by failing to report all daily cash receipts or interest and dividends.
- Overstating expenses by claiming fictitious expenses or large deductions for which no verification exists.

All of the topics discussed in this book are perfectly legal strategies and are regularly used in tax planning by Real Estate Investors.

Chapter 3
Importance of Keeping Good Records

"There is no such thing as a good tax."
Winston Churchill

This is the single most important strategy of all.

It is the foundation for implementing all of the other strategies.

Many times, I meet with real estate investors who keep sloppy records, or even no records at all. It is impossible to do any type of tax planning, if you don't have accurate, timely information about your business.

Keeping sloppy records costs you money. If you are a sloppy record keeper, I guarantee you are missing out on deductions you are LEGALLY entitled to claim.

You can't deduct expenses you haven't recorded and have documentation for. There is no way to deduct the costs that are unrecorded, undocumented, and plain just slipped-your-mind!! And if you don't deduct ALL of your expenses, you WILL overpay your taxes.

Owning a real estate investment business is a business and it should be treated as such.

Keeping good records is simply about having a filing system. As a real estate investor/landlord, you must have a basic filing system that keeps track of all of the documents you will accumulate. These include bank statements, closing statements, insurance policies, invoices for operating expenses, and real estate tax bills.

Your filing system doesn't have to be complicated. In fact, the simpler the better.

I recommend a file box for each property you own with files that separate each bill by category and by vendor.

You should open a business bank account, for each property, where you deposit all of your rents and pay all of your expenses which is separate from your personal bank account.

You can use accounting software such as QuickBooks to create a chart of accounts and set of books for tracking the activity of your real estate investment business.

For businesses that own multiple properties, I recommend setting up QuickBooks® so that it tracks income and expenses by property, using the built-in "class tracking" feature.

Alternatively, a separate QuickBooks® company file can be created and maintained for each property.

Chapter 4

Take Every Possible Legal Deduction

"The taxpayer--that's someone who works for the federal government but doesn't have to take the civil service examination."
Ronald Reagan

In many cases, Real Estate Investors do not take all of the possible legal deductions they are entitled to. There are several reasons for this:

1. Record keeping is not good enough to track all of their expenses.
2. Do not know what expenses are able to deducted against rental income.
3. They think they are less likely to be audited by the IRS if they leave legitimate, deductible, legitimate expenses off their return.

Generally, deductions against rental income can be divided into two main categories:

1. Expenses related directly to the property (Direct Property Expenses)

Direct Property expenses are expenses directly related to the ownership and operation of the property.

These items include mortgage interest, real estate taxes, insurance, repairs and maintenance, utilities, depreciation and leasing commissions.

All these expenses should be paid from a separate business checking account and tracked using an accounting system. The system need not be complex as long as it captures all expenses by property.

2. Expenses related to the Administration and Management of the property (General, Management and Administration Expenses)

Administration and management expenses are not specifically allocable to any individual property (unless you only own a single property) and includes items such as cellular and office telephone expenses, office supplies, computers and office equipment, depreciation (an accounting/tax, non-cash expenditure), internet service, marketing, postage, bank charges and any other expenses necessary for performing administrative and management duties of operating the property.

Being able to LEGALLY maximize your deductions requires that real estate investors be able to track these expenses accurately.

The better the tracking done by the investor, the more tax deductions that can be deducted and maximum tax dollars that will be saved and ultimately the more "audit-proof" the deduction and the tax return will be.

Chapter 5

Properly Classify Improvements vs. Repairs

"People try to live within their income so they can afford to pay taxes to a government that can't live within its income."
Robert Half

One of the most common mistakes relative to owning real estate investments is the misclassification between an improvement (capital expenditure) and a repair (expense item currently deductible).

While they may appear to be similar in nature, how you present and structure the facts can be the difference between a $20,000 immediate deduction or a $500 deduction every year for 40 years.

This is because all improvements/capital expenditures must be considered part of the cost basis of the property and depreciated over the useful life of the property (27.5 years for residential, 39 years for commercial).

Based on the time value of money, the larger immediate deduction is much more valuable to the real estate investor.

A dollar in your pocket today is worth much more than a dollar earned tomorrow!!!

The way it is planned out and structured can mean literally thousands of tax dollars saved and the difference in winning or losing, in the event of an IRS audit.

Improvements versus repairs is a tough question even for the IRS.

In the IRS's own Internal Manual, it states ***"it is a difficult issue requiring maximum use of judgment"***.

Here are eight powerful strategies to help ensure your repairs will be immediately deductible:

1. Segregate repairs from improvements
2. Fix a minor portion only
3. Use comparably priced materials
4. Fix damaged areas only
5. Repair after an event
6. Repair during occupancy or between tenants
7. Classify the fix-up on your books as a repair
8. If possible, try to replace less than half of any wall, ceiling or floor

How you make and document the repairs makes all the difference in getting **and maintaining** the deduction.

Ensure you have kept good records including taking date stamped photographs, logging tenant repair calls, and getting separate bills from contractors for repairs.

Remember, it is better to take the immediate deduction of the entire cost than it is to depreciate the cost over a long period of time. Understanding and using the principles of the time value of money will help you get the maximum tax breaks you deserve.

Chapter 6

Consider Using a Cost Segregation Study to Accelerate Depreciation

"You must pay taxes.
But there's no law that says you gotta leave a tip."
Morgan Stanley

Depreciation is the way in which the cost of a Real Estate Investment is expensed or written off as a business expense against rental income.

All things considered, the shorter the depreciable life of the asset the faster the asset will be expensed and the quicker the tax benefits of holding the asset will be realized.

For example, a five year asset will be depreciated over 5 years with the tax benefit being realized relatively quickly.

Single family houses are depreciated over 27 ½ years and multi-family are depreciated over 39 years.

Cost segregation studies are becoming one of the hottest tax planning strategies in real estate investing.

A Cost Segregation Study offers real estate investors a wonderful opportunity to increase cash flow and defer tax payments until later years. Yet, only the most sophisticated CPAs know much about this technique and only 15% of real estate investors have taken advantage of it.

A Cost Segregation Study (CSS) is an engineering based study that allows a real estate investor to **accelerate** a substantial amount of the depreciation deductions on a building.

This is accomplished by identifying construction or acquisition costs from the total cost of the asset that can be allocated to a shorter recovery period (depreciable life).

The basic idea is to move costs that would ordinarily be depreciated over 27.5 years (residential) or 39 years (commercial) to being depreciated over 5 to 7 years using the IRS approved, engineering based study as proof that the cost should be depreciated over a shorter life.

The shorter the depreciable life, the larger the tax deduction. The larger the tax deduction, the smaller the taxable income and thus, the lower the tax liability.

Case Study

Joe buys an apartment building in Texas for 2 million dollars in 2016.

His current accountant proposes to split the cost between land and building and depreciates the building with an allocated cost basis of 1.6 million dollars over 39 years for a 2016 depreciation deduction of $41,025.

Later in 2016, Joe hires Weinstein CPA. Weinstein suggests a Cost Segregation Study to increase his deductions and minimize his taxes. As a result of the study, 15% of the total cost of the building or $300,000 can be depreciated as 5 or 7 year property. What is the net result?

Assuming Joe has the income to offset, he can take an immediate expense deduction of $300,000 of Section 179 depreciation. The remainder of the building is depreciated over 39 years for an additional deduction of $32,000. Joe's total depreciation deduction for 2016 as a result of the Cost Segregation Study is over $332,000. This is a total difference of over $291,000 in depreciation deductions. Considering Joe's combined federal and tax rate is 35%, he saves an extra $97,000 in taxes in 2016. Not too shabby for some strategic tax planning!!!

Every real estate investor seeking to reduce their tax burden should consider this powerful strategy.

Chapter 7

Conider Using a Section 1031 Tax Free Exchanges When Selling Properties

"What is the difference between a taxidermist and a tax collector? The taxidermist takes only your skin."
Mark Twain

The Section 1031 Tax Free Exchange is the greatest tax tool for building wealth in real estate investment that exists today. While the rules are complicated and must be followed to the letter, Section 1031 allows you to sell your real estate investment and purchase another investment of equal or greater value without paying a dime in income taxes!

The basic rules of a Section 1031 Tax Free Exchange are as follows:

- The transaction must be a sale or exchange of one property for another.
- Both the property transferred and the property received must be held for either productive use in a trade or

business

- Property transferred and received must be "like-kind" yet there is little distinction between types i.e. a residential property may be exchanges for a commercial property

Additionally, it is possible to do a deferred exchange where you sell your property and purchase a replacement property. The basics of a deferred exchange are as follows:

- Upon closing of the sale of the original property, you have 45 days to identify a replacement property
- Upon closing of the sale of the original property, you have 180 days to close on the replacement property

Here is when you should elect to use a Section 1031 exchange:

- When a taxpayer intends to replace currently owned qualifying property with similar property
- When the property being disposed of has appreciated in value and a sale would result in a significant tax liability (which hopefully is the case whenever you sell a property!!)
- When a taxpayer wants to convert property from a trade or business which is actively managed to investment property

When you are selling a property that you have held as an investment, planning is essential. You have alternatives. In order to determine the best strategy for you to save on taxes, you should consult a tax professional who specializes in real estate transactions.

The success of using the Section 1031 strategy depends on the transaction being structured precisely according to the rules.

Chapter 8

Consider Using the Installment Sale Method When Selling a Property

"The wise and correct course to follow in taxation is not to destroy those who have already secured success, but to create conditions under which everyone will have a better chance to be successful."
Calvin Coolidge

Another great way to defer income taxes when selling a real estate investment is to do the accounting as an installment sale.

An installment sale transaction occurs when the seller agrees to seller-finance the property and give the buyer a mortgage.

Typically, the seller receives a down payment and then a series of mortgage payments over the life of the mortgage loan.

When a real estate investment is sold at a gain, the difference between the original purchase price of the property and the selling price is considered to be a capital gain subject to maximum income tax rates at 20%.

If no tax planning is done, the capital gain tax for the entire transaction is all due in the year of the sale, even if only a portion of the sale price(not the full amount) has been received.

However, by recording the transaction on the installment sale method, the seller only pays capital gains for the payments they received during the year. An example:

Bill bought an apartment building in 2006 for $750,000. In 2010, he sells the property for $1,000,000 getting a down payment of $200,000 and giving the buyer a mortgage at 7% interest with a 25 year amortization and a 7 year balloon payment.

Bill pays taxes on the sale as follows:

- The sales price is divided as follows – 75% return of purchase price, 25% capital gain.
- The down payment of $200,000 is divided into 2 portions - $150,000 (75%) return of purchase price and $50,000 taxable capital gain.
- Each mortgage payment is divided into 3 portions –1) taxable interest income for the interest portion of the payment, 2) the principal portion of the payment is considered to be 75% return of purchase price and 3) 25% taxable capital gain.

The beauty of using this strategy is four-fold:

- Interest income can be substantial and raises the amount of dollars received on the sale of the property.
- The capital gain on the property is split and partially deferred over a longer period of time resulting in lower total taxes paid assuming no changes in capital gains rates over the period of the loan.
- Easier to sell the property during a credit crunch
- If the buyer defaults on the mortgage, the seller can foreclose, keep the payments received including the

down payment and resell the property._

This strategy can be a win-win for the building owner who does not want to pay all of the taxes in the year of sale.

Chapter 9

Become A "Real Estate Professional"

"America is a land of taxation that was founded to avoid taxation."
Laurence J. Peter

The IRS classifies real estate investors essentially into three categories.

<u>Passive Investor</u>

The first category is that of the passive investor.

Passive investors have no management responsibility for the real estate investment. Typically this person is either a "silent partner" or could be a limited partner in larger syndicated properties.

According to IRS rules, a passive investor can only take losses on rental real estate against income on other passive income.

No net passive loss can be used to offset ordinary income such as those earned as wages or in a trade or business.

Active Participant

The second IRS classification relates to investors who "actively participate" in the management of real estate investments.

To be considered an active participant, the investor must own at least 10% of the property and be substantially involved in the management of the property. If you are considered an active participant, you are allowed to deduct up to $25,000 of rental losses against your ordinary income.

Unfortunately, the $25,000 loss can be phased out (deemed to be not deductible) for individuals or married couples whose adjusted gross income exceeds the IRS limitation. For a married couple, the active participation loss is completely non-deductible if your ordinary income exceeds $150,000 for the year.

Real Estate Professional

The third IRS classification is the best one you can have if you own real estate investments.

The classification is called "real estate professional".

Becoming a "real estate professional" requires that an individual be involved in a real estate business in which a minimum of 750 hours is expended in the business and that the hours represent at least 50% of the individual's personal services during the tax year.

Qualifying real estate businesses include those related to real property development, redevelopment, construction, acquisition, conversion, rental, operation, management, leasing or brokerage.

If you qualify, you may deduct **ALL** of your real estate losses from your real estate investments against your ordinary income.

You are now considered an Active Investor. No limitations would apply limiting passive losses only to be taken against passive income such as would happen with a passive investor.

Nor would your rental losses be limited to a net Passive Loss Deduction of $25,000 per year, as would happen with an "Active Participant".

By structuring your activities to qualify for real estate professional status, you can dramatically increase the amounts of your deductions, and the amount of losses deductible on your return and save thousands of dollars on your taxes every year.

Chapter 10

Maximize Automobile Expenses

"The purpose of a tax cut is to leave more money where it belongs: in the hands of the working men and working women who earned it in the first place."
Bob Dole

If you use your car in your real estate investment business, you can deduct expenses for the business use of your automobile.

There are two methods available for deducting auto mileage: the standard mileage allowance and the actual expense method.

You have the option of using either the standard mileage allowance or the actual expense method to calculate your deductible expenses. You can use only one of the methods in any given tax year.

Calculating business use percentage

Under the standard mileage allowance or the actual expense method, you must document your business mileage on a daily basis, detailing the number of miles driven, and the business purpose, to determine the business use percentage.

If you use your car for both business and personal purposes, you must divide your expenses between business and personal use. You can only deduct mileage incurred for business purposes.

You should calculate auto expenses under both methods to determine which method results in the larger expense and tax benefit.

Standard mileage allowance

Using the standard mileage allowance is generally considered to be the easier method of deducting automobile expenses.

The standard mileage allowance can be used instead of actual expenses. Investors who choose the standard mileage allowance may not deduct actual expenses.

If you elect to use the standard mileage allowance for a car you own, you must choose to use it in the first year the car is available for use in your business. Then in later years, you can choose to use either the standard mileage allowance or actual auto expenses.

To calculate your automobile expenses under the standard mileage allowance, you simply multiply your business miles (as calculated) by the IRS standard mileage allowance of 50 cents per mile.

Actual auto expenses

Deducting actual mileage expenses is a bit more complicated but may be worth the extra effort.

Actual auto expenses which are deductible include the cost of the vehicle and vehicle operating costs.

The cost of the vehicle includes the purchase price (which is deducted through depreciation and subject to limitations) or the lease payments paid for the vehicle (if the vehicle is leased).

Vehicle operating costs include the costs of operating the vehicle, such as fuel, insurance, repairs, and other miscellaneous costs.

The total actual expenses incurred must be multiplied by the business use percentage (see above) to determine the deductible actual auto expenses.

If actual expenses are used to calculate the deduction for a car that is leased, there are rules that affect the amount of lease payments that are deductible.

Commuting mileage

Costs related to travel between an investors home and regular place of work are commuting expenses. These are considered personal expenses and are not deductible.

Chapter 11

Take Maximum Advantage of Retirement Plans

"It's income tax time again, Americans: time to gather up those receipts, get out those tax forms, sharpen up that pencil, and stab yourself in the aorta."
Dave Barry

One of my favorite strategies to share with clients is adopting a retirement plan.

Retirement plans can be one of the best and single largest deductions available for Investors. The government actually wants you to save for your own retirement and gives you a tax deduction for saving for your golden years. (Social Security was never really meant to be a retirement account.)

Fortunately, there are many types of retirement plans available to choose from, including:

IRAs, Roth IRAs, SEP-IRAs, SIMPLE IRAs, and regular 401-Ks, Money Purchase Plans, and Profit Sharing Plans, to name just a few.

Each of these plans has unique characteristics such as its cost to establish and maintain, which employees must to be included in the plan, and the amount of the annual maximum contribution.

The appropriate plan for you would take into account the cash flow of your real estate investment business and how much you can afford to contribute; how many employees you have and whether they will need to be included in the plan, and how much will that cost; your own projected retirement needs (what is your current age, how much you will need for retirement, and how much do you have now); and of course, your tax situation (what is your incremental tax rate and how much net tax would your tax retirement plan contribution save you).

While choosing the right retirement plan for yourself and for your real estate investment business can be a very rewarding way to save money on taxes, there are many factors to consider to ensure you are making the right choices and maximize the tax savings available to you.

Chapter 12

Maximize the Home Office Deduction

"The government's view of the economy could be summed up in a few short phrases: If it moves, tax it. If it keeps moving, regulate it. And if it stops moving, subsidize it."
Ronald Reagan

As a real estate investor, you may use your home substantially and regularly to conduct business. This may qualify you to take the Home Office Deduction.

To qualify for the Home Office Deduction you must be able to pass four tests: the Exclusive Use, Regular Use, Trade or Business Use, and Principal Place of Business.

Exclusive Use

To qualify under the exclusive use test, you must use a specific area of your home only for your real estate investment business. The space does not need to marked off by a permanent partition.

The area used for business can be a room or other separately identifiable space, but must not be used for any other personal purpose. You do not meet the requirements of the exclusive use test if you use the area in question both for business and for personal purposes.

Regular Use

To qualify under the regular use test, you must use a specific area of your home for business on a regular basis. Incidental or occasional business use is not regular use. You must consider all the facts and circumstances in determining whether your use is on a regular basis.

Trade or Business Use

To qualify under the trade-or-business-use test, you must use part of your home in connection with a trade or business. If you use your home for a profit-seeking activity that is not a trade or business, you cannot take a deduction for its business use.

If you are deducting home office expenses for your real estate investment business, generally there should be no problem in meeting this test.

Principal Place of Business

To qualify for a deduction under the principal place of business test, your home must be your principal place of business. To determine if your home is your principal place of business you must consider:

- The relative importance of the activities performed at each place where you conduct business, and
- The amount of time spent at each place where you conduct business.

Your home office will qualify as your principal place of business if you meet the following requirements.

- You use it exclusively and regularly for administrative or management activities of your business, and

- You have no other fixed location where you could conduct substantial administrative or management activities of your business.

How to Deduct Home Office Expenses

If you qualify for the Home Office Deduction, you can deduct a percentage of your mortgage interest, property taxes, insurance, utilities, repairs and depreciation on your home.

Renters **would not** be able to deduct mortgage interest and property taxes. However, they **would** be able to deduct a portion of rent paid.

To calculate your deduction, you must take the total square footage of your home and divide by the area of the home used for exclusively for business. This would be the percentage of the home office expenses you can deduct on your tax return.

If you are able to take advantage of the home office deduction, you must reduce the amount of mortgage interest and real estate taxes taken as the home office deduction from the itemized deductions.

You are unable to take mortgage interest and real estate taxes as both home office deductions and itemized deductions.

Chapter 13

Tax Advantage of Employee Benefit Plans/Tax Deductible Fringe Benefits

"The politicians say 'we' can't afford a tax cut. Maybe we can't afford the politicians."
Steve Forbes

There are many ways to provide tax-free benefits. Benefits that are deductible by your real estate investment business and not taxable to you personally are always a welcome tax advantage.

Examples of non-taxable fringe benefits include:

Health and Dental Plans, expense accounts, and group term life insurance, just to name a few.

The deductibility and non-taxability of fringe benefits is dependent upon the form of business organization and whether the benefits are offered on a discriminatory basis.

The qualifications and nondiscrimination rules are different for each benefit that you are providing. Much care must be given to the selection and implementation of fringe benefits to insure maximum deductibility while still following the IRS rules and regulations.

Chapter 14

Make the Most of Meals and Entertainment Expenses

"When there's a single thief, it's robbery. When there are a thousand thieves, it's taxation."
Vanya Cohen

Meals and entertainment expenses are a perplexing area for many real estate investors.

Many investors are confused and intimidated by the rules for meals and entertainment and do not deduct expenses to which they are legitimately entitled, causing them to pay more taxes than legally required.

And the confusion experienced by some investors causes them to mistakenly either deduct expenses to which they are not legally entitled, or to deduct them at overstated amounts, which puts them at increased risk of audit.

Requirements for deductibility

Generally, the IRS allows you to take a deduction for 50 percent of your qualifying business entertainment expenses.

For meals and entertainment to qualify as deductible, one of two tests must be met, either the Directly Related Test, or the Associated Test. If you do not meet either of these tests, you cannot deduct the meals and entertainment expenses.

Directly Related Test

To meet the directly related test for entertainment expenses (including entertainment-related meals), you must be able to show that:

- The main purpose of the combined business and entertainment was for the active conduct of business, and
- You did engage in business with the person during the entertainment period, and
- You had more than a general expectation of getting income or some other specific business benefit at some future time.

You must consider all the facts, including the nature of the business transacted and the reasons for conducting business during the entertainment. It is not necessary to devote more time to business than to entertainment. However, if the business discussion is only incidental to the entertainment, the entertainment expenses do not meet the directly related test.

Associated Test

Even if your expenses do not meet the directly related test, you may be able to meet the associated test.

To qualify for the associated test for entertainment expenses (including entertainment-related meals), you must show that the entertainment is:

- Associated with the active conduct of your trade or business, and
- Directly before or after a substantial business discussion.

Associated with trade or business

Generally, an expense is associated with the active conduct of your trade or business if you can show that you had a clear business purpose for incurring the expense. The purpose may be to get new business or to encourage the continuation of an existing business relationship.

Substantial business discussion

Whether a business discussion is substantial depends on the facts of each case. A business discussion will not be considered substantial unless you can show that you actively engaged in a discussion, meeting, negotiation, or other business transaction to get income or some other specific business benefit.

The meeting does not have to be for any specified length of time. However, you must show that the business discussion was substantial in relation to the meal or entertainment. It is not necessary that you devote more time to business than to entertainment. You do not have to discuss business during the meal or entertainment.

For all meals and entertainment expenses, you must maintain adequate accounting records properly documenting the date of the expense, who was in attendance, business discussed, and the amount of the expense.

Chapter 15

Selecting the best entity for your real estate investment business

NOTE: This chapter is an adaptation of one of my other books, ***"The Official Business Owner's Guide to Selecting a Business Entity-How Every New and Existing Business Can Choose the Best Entity to Operate Their Business"***

"Be thankful we're not getting all the government we're paying for."
Will Rogers

Every entity from which you can choose has both tax and non-tax aspects that need to be considered when selecting an entity in which to do business.

Tax considerations include how income is taxed, what taxes are involved, and who is responsible for reporting and paying the tax, among other things.

Non-tax considerations include how many owners the business can have, the legal standing of the business, legal liability exposure of the business owners, the legal life of the business, and the non-taxable benefits available to the owners.

There are six structures available under which you can operate your business: a Sole Proprietorship, a General Partnership, a Limited Partnership, a C Corporation, an S Corporation, or a Limited Liability Company.

Sole Proprietorship/Individual Investor

What is a Sole Proprietorship/ Individual Investor? By definition, a sole proprietorship/individual investor is an unincorporated business which is owned by a single investor.

Ownership. A sole proprietorship/individual investor can ***only*** be owned by a single person. A person is defined as an individual, not another entity such as a corporation or a partnership.

A business owned by more than one investor cannot be operated as a sole proprietorship/individual investor. Some other form of business entity that allows multiple owners must be used.

Ease of formation. A sole proprietorship/individual investor is the easiest business entity to form. All an investor must do is: declare you are open for business, and begin business operations. It is generally a good idea to register your business name with the appropriate authority to ensure no one else is using the business name, and to reserve your right to use the selected name.

No formal legally recognized entity. No formal separate legal entity is required. Thus, there is no legal separation between the proprietor/investor and the business. The income and personal assets of the business owners are treated as those of the sole proprietorship.

Even though there is no formal legal separation of business assets from personal assets, it is suggested your business be operated from a business checking account, separate and distinct from your personal checking account.

This makes the accounting process much easier, as all business transactions are segregated from your personal transactions. Additionally, this can potentially limit the IRS looking at personal transactions in the event of an audit.

Tax reporting

No separate tax filing is required for a sole proprietorship/ individual investor. The net income or loss of the investor is reported on Schedule E, "Supplemental Income and Loss", which is a separate detailed schedule included on the owner's Federal Income Tax Return (Form 1040).

How is income allocated?

Since there is only one owner as an individual investor, there is no allocation of income. All of the income is reported by the investor.

Tax paying

The investor pays tax on their personal tax return, Form 1040, Schedule E "Supplemental Income and Loss".

What taxes are involved?

The business's net income is subject to federal income tax. The income of the business is considered rental income, and is NOT subject to self-employment tax.

How is the investor paid?

The investor is paid by taking a distribution of profits. Since all the profits of the business already belong to the investor, the investor simply needs to write a check to himself. This is known as an owner's draw.

Draws are not an expense of the business, and do not serve to reduce taxable income. They are simply how the investor chooses to distribute the profits.

Advantages of a Sole Proprietorship/Individual Investor

Very easy to set up—All you need to do is to begin doing business. No formal organization or legal paperwork is required. The IRS is notified of your intention to form a sole proprietorship when you file your tax return and include a Schedule E, on April 15 of the year following the end of your first year of business.

Simplified payroll—There is no need to set up the investor as an employee and write a payroll check, or deal with additional responsibilities such as quarterly payroll tax filings, paying employment taxes, and preparing an annual W-2.

Note: Regardless of the type of entity chosen, if a business has employees, it must meet and follow additional requirements which are beyond the scope of this book.

"Pass-through" of losses—Losses "pass through" to the investors personal tax return. These losses can be used to offset any other taxable income of the owner, subject to certain limitations. This can be important if the business will be generating losses at the inception of the business.

Tax reporting is simplified—Income and expenses of the investment business are reported on the tax return of the investor. No separate tax returns for the investment business need to be prepared.

Of course, if the investor hires employees, they must comply with all recordkeeping and filing requirements for their employees.

Disadvantages of a Sole Proprietorship/Individual

Single owner—A sole proprietorship/individual investor can only have one owner. If more than one owner is desired, another form of entity must be used.

Taxed on income—The investor is personally responsible for the tax due on the profits of the business, regardless of whether or not cash was taken out of the business.

Unlimited personal liability—The investor is subject to unlimited personal liability. The investor is personally liable for all debts and other liabilities and judgments of the business, even if in excess of the amount invested or loaned to the business.

Not only are the assets of the business at risk, but all assets personally owned by the investor are also subject to the risks of the business.

Difficulty raising capital—It can be much tougher raising capital as an individual investor. Capital used in a sole proprietorship/individual investor is limited to the personal funds contributed by the investor and the ability of the investor to borrow.

Assets of the investor will serve as the primary collateral for loans, which may not be enough for some lenders.

Additionally, the creditworthiness of the investor will be analyzed in making a credit decision.

No continuity of life—Since a sole proprietorship/individual is owned by a single individual, when this individual dies, the business technically ceases to exist. Their heirs may be able to sell the business, but it may be more difficult.

Who Should Operate as a Sole Proprietorship/Individual?

A sole proprietorship/individual investor is usually considered by individuals with businesses that are just beginning operations.

Ease of formation and minimal legal expenses are a big plus.

There are no expenses of formation, other than registering the business name. If a business is being started on a limited budget, a sole proprietorship/individual may be a good choice.

Many new businesses are not profitable in the first year and generate losses. Losses that are generated by a sole proprietorship/individual can be used by the investor to offset taxable income from other sources such as a working spouse, other rental properties, investment income or other employment, subject to certain limitations.

Who Should Not Operate as a Sole Proprietorship/Individual Investor

Since sole proprietors/individual investors can only have a single owner, if there will be more than one owner, another entity must be considered.

Be aware that sole proprietors/individual investors are responsible for the financial obligations of the business. Additionally, the investors personal assets are at risk for any business debts or court judgments.

If there could be significant liability exposure, it may be wise to consider another type of entity that will limit the investors liability.

General Partnership

What is a General Partnership? A general partnership is an association that is owned by two or more persons to conduct business as co-owners for a profit.

"Persons" is defined as individuals, partnerships, corporations, and limited liability companies (much broader than a sole proprietor).

Ownership. A general partnership is owned by two or more persons. There is no limit to the number of persons who can be owners of a general partnership.

All partners can act as an agent of the partnership for the purpose of conducting its business. All partners are legally bound by the actions of any partner who acts within the scope of the partnership's business.

A single person cannot own a general partnership. A single individual must operate as either a sole proprietor or a single-member limited liability company, a C corporation, or an S corporation

Ease of formation. Like a sole proprietorship, a general partnership is also a relatively easy business entity to form. All the owners need to do is declare they are open for business and to begin operations.

It is generally a good idea to register the business name with the local authority to ensure no one is using the name and to reserve your right to use the selected name.

It is also suggested that a partnership agreement be adopted and signed by all of the partners.

Items that should be included in the agreement:

- The term of the partnership
- How changes to the partnership ownership will be handled upon the death, disability, retirement or withdrawal of a partner
- Requirements for the admission of new partners
- How income/losses will be allocated
- How and when partner distributions will be made and how they will be determined
- What the capital contributions of the partners will be and how the partner interests will be divided
- Listing of duties and responsibilities of the partners
- How the partnership will handle management of the partnership

The personal assets of the partners are treated as available for the settlement of partnership debts. There is no separation between the assets of the partners and the assets of the partnership. Basically, if the partnership gets sued, then the assets of the partners are at risk.

Legal liability

All partners in a general partnership are jointly and severally liable for the actions of their partners and also for the debts, obligations and liabilities of the partnership.

Joint and several liability means that a creditor can pursue any or all partners to collect on debts. Generally, creditors can pursue ALL partners, to try and obtain a settlement, since there is no formal legal separation of partnership assets from a partner's personal assets.

It is suggested that a partnership maintain a business checking account, separate and distinct from the personal checking accounts of the partners.

Tax reporting

A separate tax filing is required for a general partnership. The activities of the general partnership are reported on a Form 1065, "U. S. Return of Partnership Income." Allocable partner income or loss is reported to the partners on Schedule K-1, "Partner's Share of Income, Deductions and Credits."

How is income allocated?

Income is allocated on a pro-rata basis (based upon ownership) among the partners. Generally, the net income or losses are allocated to the partners based upon the ownership percentages, unless the partnership agreement indicates otherwise.

However, a general partnership is very flexible in how income and losses can be allocated to the partners. Income and losses are not required to be allocated based upon the percentage ownership of the partners. Income and losses can be allocated to partners in any manner in which they agree, as long as the allocation has real economic effect and is not being done to evade taxes.

For example, all of the losses can be allocated to one partner and all of the profits can be allocated to another partner. Or an allocation can be made on a 75/25% basis, when in fact, there are only two partners who each own 50%.

The only requirement is that the entire amount of income or loss be allocated to someone and that evasion of tax is not the reason for the allocation.

Tax paying

The general partnership is a tax reporting, but not a tax paying entity. Income is allocated to each individual partner, who must report and pay taxes on their pro-rata portion of the income or loss on their personal tax return.

What taxes are involved?

The partner's reported net income is subject to federal income tax. Because the income of the general partners is considered rental income, it is NOT subject to self-employment tax.

How are the owners paid?

A partner can receive two types of income from the partnership: guaranteed payments and cash distributions.

Partners can be paid *guaranteed payments* from the partnership for their efforts. Guaranteed payments to partners are an expense of the partnership and reduce the net income of the partnership, and the amount of income reported to the partners. Guaranteed payments to partners are reported on Schedule K-1, and also have to be reported on a W-2.

Partners can also receive *cash distributions* from the partnership. Partnership distributions are usually considered to be a distribution of income, similar to owner draws taken by a sole proprietor.

Accordingly, partnership distributions are not considered income to the shareholder and are not subject to self-employment tax.

Partners can have distributions made in any amount agreed to by the partners, subject to cash availability.

Partnership distributions up to the amount of the partners' capital account are considered a return of capital and are not taxable.

Distributions in excess of the balance in their partners' capital account would be reported as capital gain income.

Advantages of a General Partnership

Relatively easy to set up—All that a general partnership must do is to begin operations. No formal organization or legal paperwork is required.

A newly formed general partnership must obtain an Employer Identification Number (EIN) by completing Form SS-4, "Application for Employer Identification Number." This identifying number will be used by the partnership on all of their tax filings.

Multiple owners—By definition, a general partnership must consist of two or more partners (owners). An unlimited number of partners can be in a general partnership.

Easier to raise capital—Having more than one partner can allow multiple partners to contribute capital to the business and have the ability to borrow money on behalf of the business. It may be easier to get a loan with more people signing as responsible parties.

More depth of management—Having more than one owner diversifies the management talent available to the business. The more partners involved, the more talent, experience, and skill-sets available to help grow and run the business.

Simplified payroll—Partners are not employees so there are no payroll tax filings, employment taxes and no need to prepare annual W-2s.

Of course, if the partnership hires employees, the partnership must comply with all recordkeeping and filing requirements for their employees.

"Pass-through" of losses—Losses "pass through" to the partner's personal tax return. This can be important if the partnership is generating losses. These losses can be used to offset any other taxable income of the partner, subject to the following limitations.

No double taxation of profits—Since a partnership is not a tax paying entity, tax is only paid by the individual partners. All profits flow through to the partners who pay their portion of the tax on their personal tax returns.

Disadvantages of a General Partnership

More management—Although many may consider having more partners and the additional talent that goes along with more partners as an asset, this may not always be the case.

Human nature will always come into play. Sometimes disagreements will arise concerning business decisions that can be tough to settle.

Complaints about money and draws—There can be major disagreements between the partners concerning money. This can be the single largest problem faced by general partnerships. More partnerships break up over money than all other reasons combined.

Reasons for disagreements can include uneven distributions of profit based upon capital contributed, effort expended or results achieved.

A well-drafted partnership agreement should thoroughly address how partnership distributions will be handled.

Taxed on income—Partners are personally responsible for the tax due on their pro-rata profits of the business, regardless of whether cash was distributed from the business.

However, it is quite common for the partnership to make

distributions to the partners (which are not considered income) to cover the tax liability incurred by the partners, attributable to partner income.

Unlimited personal liability—Partners are subject to unlimited personal liability. All partners are personally liable for all debts and liabilities and judgments of the partnership. This includes any actions taken by any other partners on behalf of the partnership.

This may the single biggest disadvantage of a general partnership.

Difficulty raising capital—It can be tough raising capital as a partnership. The assets of the partners and the partnership serve as the primary collateral for loans, which may not satisfy some lenders' requirements.

No continuity of life—A general partnership is owned by the partners. When there is a 50% or greater change in ownership, the partnership technically ceases to exist. A new partnership must be established for the remaining partners, which would entail additional paperwork and possible legal fees.

Who is a General Partnership Best Suited For?

A general partnership might be considered by individuals with businesses that are just commencing operations.

Many new businesses are not profitable in the first year or two, and generate losses that can be used by the partners to reduce their taxable income from other sources of income such as a working spouse, other rental properties, or investment income.

If there will be more than one owner, the owners may want to consider a general partnership. If there will be only one owner, another entity must be considered.

There are no expenses of formation, other than registering the business name. A general partnership is a good choice if the owners are working with a limited budget.

Who Should Not Operate as a General Partnership

If there is significant potential for liability exposure in your chosen real estate investment business, you may want to consider another form of business with limited liability exposure for the owners, such as a corporation or limited liability company.

Potential liability exposure could include anything from someone slipping and falling on your property to an employee suing you.

Be aware that all general partners are responsible for all financial obligations of the business. Additionally, the partner's personal assets are at risk for any business debts or court judgments. If being held responsible for the actions of your partner(s) concerns you, you may want to consider a different type of entity.

I suggest that you know your partners very well before going into business with them. Because you will be held responsible for the actions of your partner, you should ensure that any potential partners are trustworthy and exercise good judgment. Make sure, and do a thorough background check on your partner. Hopefully, you'll know the people you're going into business with.

Ideally, you should find a partner who brings a different set of skills to the business than you do. For example, if you are exceptionally talented in marketing, choose a partner with complementary skills such as finance or operations.

The truth contained in an age-old saying, "Two heads are better than one," can be very helpful in a small business partnership.

Finally, having a buy-sell agreement already in place will help the partners amicably end the partnership when they decide to do so.

Limited Partnership

A limited partner is a partnership which is formed by two or more persons. A limited partner has some attributes of a general partnership and some attributes of a corporation.

There must be at least one or more general partners. There can be one or more limited partners.

General partners are responsible for managing the partnership's business activities. General partners have unlimited liability for all debts and obligations of the partnership.

Limited partners are generally only liable for the amount of their initial capital contribution/investment and any subsequent investments.

Limited partners are **not** liable for the debts and obligations of the limited partnership.

Limited partners should not in any way participate in management. If a limited partner participates in management, or is significantly involved in the operations of the business, they may lose their limited liability protection.

The formation and operation of a limited partnership requires more formality than does the formation and operation of a general partnership.

Generally, a limited partnership must file a certificate of limited partnership with the Secretary of State and must have a written partnership agreement. These documents govern the business operations of the entity. A written partnership agreement is strongly suggested.

Tax reporting

Similar to a general partnership, a separate tax filing is required for a limited partnership. The net income or loss of the limited partnership is reported on Form 1065, "U. S. Return of Partnership Income." Partner income or loss is reported to the partners on Schedule K-1, "Partner's Share of Income, Deductions and Credits."

How is income allocated?

Income is allocated on a pro-rata basis among the partners, based upon the ownership percentages.

However, a limited partnership is very flexible in how income and losses can be allocated to the partners. Income and losses are not required to be allocated based upon the percentage ownership of the partners. Income and losses can be allocated to partners in any manner in which they agree, as long as the allocation has real economic effect and is not being done to evade taxes.

For example, all of the losses can be allocated to one partner and all of the profits can be allocated to another partner. Or an allocation can be made on a 75/25 % basis, when in fact, there are only two partners who each own 50%. The only requirement is that the entire amount of income or loss be allocated to someone and that evasion of tax is not the reason for the allocation.

Tax paying

A limited partnership is a tax reporting, not a tax paying, entity. Income is allocated to each individual partner, who then report and pay taxes on their pro-rata portion of the income on their personal tax return.

What taxes are involved?

For all partners, the reported net income is subject to federal income tax.

Rental income/loss is not subject to self-employment tax for the general or limited partners.

How are the owners paid?

A partner can receive two types of income from the partnership. The general partner can be paid "guaranteed payments to partners" for effort expended, analogous to wages.

Guaranteed payments to general partners are an expense of the partnership and reduce the net income of the partnership, and the amount of income reported to the partners. Guaranteed payments to partners are reported on the partner's Schedule K-1.

Since limited partners cannot actively participate in the operation of the business, they cannot be paid guaranteed payments for the services they perform.

Partners can also receive cash distributions from the partnership. Partnership distributions are usually considered to be a distribution of income, similar to owner draws for a sole proprietor.

Partners can have distributions made in any amount agreed to by the partners, subject to cash availability.

Partnership distributions up to the amount of the partner's capital account are considered a return of capital and not taxable. Partnership distributions that are in excess of the balance in their capital account would be reported as capital gain income and are taxable.

Advantages of a Limited Partnership

Multiple owners—There can be an unlimited number of owners. The only requirement is that there must be at least one general partner and at least one limited partner.

Usually, there is only one general partner, but there can be more.

The number of limited partners is usually only limited by the amount of money needed by the partnership.

Limited liability—Limited partners' liability exposure is limited to their investment in the partnership. Limited partners are not liable for the debts and general obligations of the partnership.

Limited partners should not participate in management or perform significant personal services for the partnership.

Partnership distributions—Partners may receive cash distributions without affecting their tax liability.

Partners are liable for the tax on their *pro-rata* share of the partnership's profits, whether or not they are distributed.

At a minimum many partnerships distribute enough money to allow the partners to pay for the partners' taxes on the partnership income.

Centralized management—Management is centralized under the control of the general partner. Limited partners are not and should not be involved in the operations of the business. Limited partners basically serve as investors only.

Raising capital—There is no limit to the number of limited partners. The amount of capital raised by the limited partnership is only limited by the number of limited partners that can be recruited for the capital requirements of the limited partnership.

This can be one of the main reasons for using a limited partnership to raise money for real estate investments businesses requiring large investments.

Continuity of life—Unlike general partnerships, most limited partnerships don't terminate on the death or disability of a limited partner.

However, if a general partner dies or becomes disabled, this could become a problem unless the partnership agreement allows limited partners to recruit or assign a new general partner.

"Pass-through" of income—Partnerships are tax reporting and not tax paying. Income and losses of the partnerships are "passed through" to the partners who pay tax at their individual rates. Losses can be used to offset other taxable income of the partners, subject to certain limitations.

Disadvantages of a Limited Partnership

Limited marketability—There usually isn't a strong secondary market for limited partnership interests. This can make the sale of a limited partnership interest difficult.

Usually, in the cases of privately-held limited partnerships, the only people interested in buying your partnership interest are the other limited partners and/or the general partner. (If it's a publicly traded limited partnership, the scenario would be different.)

Normally, the general partner must approve the sale of a partnership interest to another party.

Unlimited liability for the general partner—The general partner has unlimited liability for the debts and obligations of the limited partnership.

One of the ways around this is that the general partner can be organized as either a corporation or a limited liability company, which enjoy limited liability protection.

More costly to organize and administer—Because most people usually consult an attorney to help set this up, it is frequently costly to establish a limited partnership due to the filing of "Certificate of Limited Partnership" and the complexity of the partnership agreement, and the requirement for good accounting and proper tax reporting to the partners.

No control over the general partner—General partners control the day-to-day activities of the partnership. Limited partners have little control over how the general partner operates the business.

Limited partners may not participate in management—If limited partners participate in management they may lose their limited liability status. Businesses which require the personal services of limited partners should consider other types of entities.

Passive loss limitations—Limited partnerships are generally treated as passive activities. You may be limited as an individual in how much or whether you will be able to deduct the losses generated by your partnership interest.

Passive losses can only be offset against passive income. "Passive activities" are those in which you're generally not involved in the operations of the business yourself, but where you are an "investor" instead. If your passive losses are limited, then they are written off against passive income, or they can be carried over to subsequent years when you might be able to utilize them, or until the investment is sold or otherwise disposed of.

Who is a Limited Partnership Best Suited For?

Limited partnerships can be very useful entities. They limit the liability of limited partners and can be used to raise significant amounts of capital. However, limited partners can not be actively involved in the business.

Real estate investment businesses can effectively utilize limited partnerships. This is because limited partners can make an investment and not be subject to all the underlying liabilities involved in owning and running the partnership.

Again, a limited partner of the business may not be directly involved with running the business, because this is being done by the general partner.

Who Should Not Use a Limited Partnership?

Limited partnerships should not be used by entities in which all partners render services to the business or will be actively involved in the management of the business.

Active participation by limited partners in their businesses will nullify their limited liability status.

C Corporation

A corporation is a legal entity, formed under state law, that exists separate and apart from its owners and shareholders.

The word *incorporate* means to create a "separate body." Corporations have all the rights and powers of a "natural person" (as opposed to a "fictitious person"), including the right to conduct lawful business, to own property, to enter into contracts, to be responsible for its own debts, and to sue and be sued in its corporate name.

Corporations are a "fictitious person" that are granted their legal status by filing the appropriate legal documents such as the Articles of Incorporation and by-laws with the Secretary of State in the state of organization.

Since the business is a separate legal entity, owners of the business, called shareholders, have legal liability protection.

Generally, all debts and obligations of the corporation remain exclusively with the corporation, and not the shareholders. The liability of the shareholders is limited to the amount of money invested into the corporation.

A corporation, by default, is called a C corporation. C corporations are named after Subchapter C of the Internal Revenue Code.

Tax reporting

A C corporation is a tax reporting and tax paying entity. A separate tax filing is required for a C corporation. The net income or loss of a C corporation is reported on a Form 1120, "U.S. Corporation Income Tax Return."

How is income allocated?

There is no income allocation for a C corporation, such as with "pass-through" entities. All income of the corporation is the responsibility of the corporation.

Tax paying

A C corporation reports and pays taxes on 100% of its income. Losses not tax deductible currently by the corporation are carried forward or backward to offset profits.

What taxes are involved?

A C corporation's reported net income is subject to Federal Corporate Income Tax. This corporate income tax is separate from the federal income tax paid by the shareholders on their individual income tax return and is not the responsibility of the shareholders.

How is the owner paid?

A shareholder/owner of the corporation can receive two types of income from the corporation. Shareholders can be paid wages from the corporation, just like any other employee.

If a shareholder works for and provides services for a C corporation, they are an employee of the corporation and must be paid wages for the services that they perform.

Wages paid to shareholders are an expense of the corporation and reduce the net income of the corporation. Wages paid to shareholders are reported on a Form W-2, just like wages paid to any other employee.

Shareholders can also receive dividends from the corporation. Dividends paid to shareholders are considered to be a distribution of retained earnings and are not tax deductible by the corporation. However, dividends are considered income to the shareholder and included in the shareholder's taxable income, thus causing double taxation, once at the corporate level and once at the shareholder level.

Advantages of a C Corporation

Limited liability—The single greatest non-tax reason to establish a corporation is limited liability protection.

When the corporation is properly set up and the owners adhere to the corporate formalities, a shareholder's liability is limited to their investment in the corporation. Because a corporation is a *fictitious person*, it is responsible for its own debts and obligations. They are not debts and obligations of the shareholders.

Reasons for losing the limited liability status of the corporation include fraud, malpractice, and failure to adhere to the corporate formalities, such as having annual shareholder meetings and documenting these meetings in the corporate minutes.

Transferability of ownership—Unlike general partnerships or limited partnerships, an owner in a C corporation can usually sell his or her stock without the approval of the corporation or other stockholders. However, in many non-public small corporations, shareholder agreements are in place which may restrict the transfer of shares.

Continuity after the death of shareholders/owners—If a shareholder dies, the corporation continues to exist. Generally, the heirs of the shareholder will inherit their shares, or they will pass in accordance with the deceased's will.

Ease of raising capital—If you need to raise additional cash for your business, you can sell authorized, but previously unissued, shares of stock in your C corporation to outside investors. These investors are investing money in your business, but may not normally be involved in the operations of the business.
Large businesses traded on a national stock exchange are usually organized as C corporations and can sell as many shares to the public as are authorized.

Specialized management—Corporations may hire as many officers and managers as they can afford. A corporation can hire people to handle many different aspects of the business, such as finance, marketing, and operations.

Accumulation of capital—Unlike pass-through entities, corporations are subject to their own tax rates. This allows corporations to pay tax on their earnings and accumulate capital within the corporation. There is no requirement for a corporation to pay a dividend.

Capital can be accumulated for any valid business purpose such as expansion of the business, purchase of inventory, or marketing.

Tax-free benefits for employees—Employees of C corporations can receive fringe benefits on a tax-free basis. These benefits can include health insurance, disability insurance, and group term life insurance up to $50,000.

Ordinary loss on sale of stock—If planned correctly during the formation of the corporation, you can elect for the stock in your corporation to be classified as small business stock (section 1244). Losses realized on the sale of small business stock are considered ordinary losses, and can be written off directly against any other income of the shareholder in the year of the loss.

Normally, losses on the sale of stock (capital losses) are limited to a net capital loss deduction of $3,000 per year. Any losses greater than $3,000 must be carried forward to future years to be deducted, with the same $3,000 per year limitation.

The requirements to qualify as Small Business Stock are as follows:

1. The stock was issued by a domestic corporation which was a "small business corporation" at the time the stock was issued;

2. The stock was issued by such corporation for money or other property (other than stock and securities); and

3. The aggregate amount received for the stock was less than one million dollars; and

4. The corporation, during the period of its five most recent taxable years ending before the date the loss on such stock was sustained, derived more than 50% of its aggregate gross receipts from sources other than royalties, rents, dividends, interests, annuities, and sales or exchanges of stocks or securities.

Exclusion of gain on small business stock—Shareholders of small business stock may exclude up to 50% of the gain they realize on the disposition of their stock. To qualify, the stock must have been issued after August 10, 1993 and held by the shareholder for more than five years.

Disadvantages of a C Corporation

Double taxation—C corporations report and pay their own taxes. This tax must be paid by the corporation. Dividends paid out to shareholders are taxed to the shareholders as dividend income when received. This is considered "double taxation."

Some business owners reduce their corporate income (and corporate income tax) to zero, by monitoring the income at year end, and paying out enough in bonus and salaries to the owners to reduce the corporate income tax to zero.

This serves to reduce corporate income tax and shifts the income tax to the shareholder and mitigates "double taxation" of corporate income.

In some instances, it may be beneficial to incur the "double taxation" by taking advantage of the lower corporate tax rates. For example, if a corporation is in a lower tax bracket than an individual, then the tax to the corporation would be less. Ultimately, I still consider this to be "double taxation," and I don't see it done very often in the real world.

All of this takes proper accounting and planning, which increases the costs of maintaining the corporation.

No "pass-through" of losses—Because the corporation is a separate tax reporting and tax paying entity, any losses generated by the corporation can only be used by the corporation. There is no tax benefit to the shareholders.

Losses do not "pass through" to the shareholders to be used to offset their personal income. Thus, in the early years of the business or in years in which the business generates a loss, there is no tax benefit to the shareholders/owners for losses generated.

Additional paperwork—Properly operating a C corporation involves much additional paperwork. Corporate formalities that must be addressed include annual shareholder meetings, board meetings to elect officers, and approval of major issues within the corporation such as debt, and approval of major purchases and business strategies. These must all be formally documented in the corporate minutes.

Additionally, separate and distinct bank accounts in the corporation's name must be maintained for the corporation, as well as a proper accounting system and books and records.

More expensive to form—A corporation must pay its Secretary of State an incorporation fee to be established.

Added administrative costs—Operating a corporation involves preparing a corporate income tax return, including all of the accounting required to prepare the return. A corporation has employees, which involves preparing payroll, and preparing quarterly and annual payroll reports.

Potential tax issues—Corporations have many potential traps established to defeat potential abuses by taxpayers.

Additional taxes can be assessed for:

- Personal holding companies—Corporations with excessive unearned income such as interest, dividends and capital gains.
- Accumulated earnings tax—Corporations with excessive accumulated earnings that have not been paid out in dividends.
- Personal service corporations—Corporations which render personal services such as medicine, law, accounting, engineering and consulting are assessed a flat 35% tax on all income.

Who Should Operate as a C Corporation?

Real estate investors who have significant potential liability exposure and desire to protect themselves.

Real estate investors that need to accumulate capital for inventory, marketing, and expansion.

Real estate investors that expect to go public sometime in the future.

Real estate investors that want tax deductible fringe benefits including health insurance.

Who Should Not Operate as a C Corporation

Real estate investors that determine they do not need limited liability protection.

Real estate investors that cannot afford the cost of incorporation, the cost of accounting, and the additional costs of maintaining the corporate documents.

S Corporation

S corporations are corporations organized just like C corporations. They are granted their legal status (known as a charter) by the Secretary of State in their state of incorporation. S corporations have the same corporate formalities as C corporations such as stockholder meetings, board of directors meetings, and the keeping of corporate minutes.

However, an S corporation is a hybrid entity. It has the limited liability structure of a corporation, but it is taxed like a partnership. S corporations are named after Subchapter S of the Internal Revenue Code.

S corporation status must be elected after forming the entity by filing a Form 2553, "Election by a Small Business Corporation." This election must be agreed to and signed by all shareholders.

The qualification for being an S corporation are:

- The corporation must have 100 or fewer shareholders. A husband and wife count as only one shareholder.
- The corporation must be a domestic corporation formed in the United States. Corporations formed in other countries cannot elect S status.

- Only individuals, estates and certain types of limited trusts can be shareholders. Partnerships, other corporations and most trusts can't own stock in an S corporation.

- All stock must be owned by a U.S. resident or U.S. citizen. Foreign investors are not allowed.

- There can be only a single class of stock. If you have more than one class of stock, you can't be an S corporation.

You must meet *all* of the above requirements at the time the S corporation election is made, and continue to meet them to be an S corporation.

If you meet all five requirements at the inception of the business, and violate even one of the requirements at any time in the future, your S corporation status terminates on the date of the violation.

Since all business is conducted in the name of the corporation, owners of the business, called shareholders, have limited liability protection. All debts and obligations of the corporation remain exclusively with the corporation, and not the shareholders. The liability of the shareholders is limited to the amount of money invested in the corporation and any debts personally guaranteed.

Tax reporting
A separate tax filing is required for an S corporation. The net income or loss of an S corporation is reported on a Form 1120S, "U.S. Income Tax Return for an S Corporation."

How is income allocated?
Income is allocated on a pro-rata basis among the shareholders. The net income or losses are allocated to the shareholders, based upon ownership percentages. There is no flexibility in the allocation of profit and loss.

Tax paying
An S corporation is a tax reporting, but not a tax paying entity.

No tax is paid by the corporation. The income is allocated to each individual shareholder, who each report and pay taxes on the pro-rata portion of their income on their personal tax return.

What taxes are involved?
Shareholders pay Federal Income Tax and Social Security on all wages they receive.

Income allocated to the shareholders is not considered self-employment income, and is not subject to self-employment tax.

How is the owner paid?
A shareholder/owner of an S corporation can receive two types of income from the corporation. Shareholders can be paid wages from the corporation, like any other employee.

If a shareholder works for and provides services for an S corporation, they are an employee of the corporation and must be paid wages for the services that they perform.

Wages paid to shareholders are reported on a Form W-2, similar to wages paid to any other employee.

Wages paid to shareholders are an expense of the corporation and reduce the net income of the corporation.

Shareholders may also receive shareholder distributions from the S corporation. Shareholder distributions are made in accordance with the shareholder's percentage of ownership.

Shareholder cash distributions are considered to be a distribution of income and are not a tax deductible expense of the corporation.

Shareholder cash distributions are not considered income to the shareholder and are not subject to self-employment tax.

Advantages of an S Corporation

No double taxation—S corporations report their own income, however the taxes are paid by shareholders on their personal returns. There is no income tax at the corporate level, such as with a C corporation.

Continuity of life—If a shareholder of an S corporation dies, the S corporation continues to exist. There is no need to reform the corporation upon the death of the shareholder. Generally, the heirs of the shareholder would receive their shares through inheritance,or they will pass in accordance with the will.

"Pass-through" of losses—Losses "pass through" to the shareholders based upon their pro-rata share of stock ownership and can be used to offset other income of the shareholder.

Shareholders are compensated for their work with wages—If a shareholder works in the business, they must be paid fair and reasonable wages for the work performed. These wages are considered earned income and are taxable to the shareholder. This earned income can qualify you for participation in a retirement plan which is based on earned income.

Shareholders can receive cash distributions—Shareholders can be paid a profit distribution, commonly called a shareholder's distribution. Shareholders' distributions are not a deductible expense of the corporation, and do not reduce corporate income nor are they taxable income to the shareholder.

It is common for S corporations to make cash distributions to the shareholders at least in the amount of tax paid by the shareholder on their pro-rata share of the corporate income.

Limited liability—S corporations have the same limited liability protection as C corporations. Of course all legal formalities must be adhered to such as board meetings, shareholder meetings, and the keeping of corporate records.

Easier accounting and tax planning—Because there is no

tax at the corporate level, the double taxation involved with C corporations is eliminated. This elimination of one level of tax makes planning simpler.

Ordinary loss on sale of stock—Similar to a C corporation, an election can be made for the stock in your corporation to be classified as small business stock (section 1244).

Losses on the sale of small business stock are considered an ordinary loss, and can be written off directly against any other income of the shareholder in the year of the loss, rather than the limitation of the net capital loss deduction of $3,000 per year.

See C corporations for requirements of being classified Section 1244 Small Business Stock.

Ability to split income—Income is allocated to shareholders based upon their pro-rata share of stock ownership. Having family members who are in lower tax brackets become co-owners of the business may allow some income to be taxed at their lower rates, thereby lowering income tax payments.

Exclusion of gain on small business stock—Shareholders of small business stock may exclude up to 50% of the gain they realize on the disposition of their stock. To qualify, the stock must have been issued after August 10, 1993, and held by the shareholder for more than five years.

Specialized management—Similar to a C corporation, S corporations can also have centralized management. All Corporations have a board of directors whose job is to oversee management on behalf of the shareholders.

Less potential for tax traps—Because an S corporation is a "pass-through" entity and does not have its own tax rates nor pay its own tax as a C corporation does, it is less likely to encounter the tax problems that are possible with C corporations. Some of these problems can include being classified as a Personal Services Corporation or a Personal Holding Company, or having the Accumulated Earnings Tax assessed.

Disadvantages of an S Corporation

Restrictions on qualifying for S corporation status—

There are restrictions that must be met to qualify as an S corporation. If you don't meet these requirements at the inception of the business, or at any time in the future, a business cannot operate as an S corporation and the election will be terminated.

Increased accounting cost—An accurate accounting must be made to prepare the corporate tax return and to properly allocate income and expense to the shareholders.

Additional paperwork—Because an S corporation is a legal corporation, operating an S corporation involves additional paperwork, as does a C corporation.

Corporate formalities that must be addressed include annual shareholders meetings, board meetings to elect officers, and approval of major issues within the corporation such as debt and approval of major purchases and business strategies. These must all be formally documented in the corporate minutes.
"Pass-through" of earnings—Because an S corporation is a "pass-through" entity, capital cannot be accumulated at lower corporate tax rates within the corporation, as can be done with a C corporation.

Phantom income—The pro rata share of S corporation income is taxed to shareholders whether or not they received the cash. At a minimum, shareholder distributions should be made to the shareholders to cover the tax paid on behalf of the S corporation.

Less ability to raise capital—Because of the limitation on the number of shareholders allowed, an S corporation is limited to whatever assets the allowed shareholders can contribute.

Limitations on fringe benefits—Generally, fringe benefits such as health insurance are includable in the wages of the shareholders, rather than being treated as a business expense.

Distributions of profit—Distributions of profit must be made in the same proportion as ownership interest. No other type of allocation is permitted, such as with a general partnership which can generally allocate the profits and losses amongst the partners as desired.

Who Should Operate as an S Corporation?

Businesses that are looking for limited liability protection.

Businesses that can afford the cost of incorporating and the ongoing cost of accounting and the cost of maintaining corporate documents.

Businesses that will be generating losses at the corporate level. These losses can be used by shareholders to reduce other income on their personal tax return, subject to certain limitations. Deductible losses are limited to the shareholder's basis in the stock.

Businesses that are concerned about the possibility of double taxation. There is no tax at the corporate level for S corporations. All S corporation income is taxed at the individual shareholder level. Thus, there is little need to monitor the income of the corporation at year-end to determine if it is necessary to pay additional salary or bonuses to the shareholders to reduce the Corporate Income Tax.

Businesses that wish to split income between family members in lower tax brackets. Having family members who are in lower tax brackets own shares in the corporation shifts income and lower taxes.

Who Should Not Operate as an S Corporation?

Businesses that have more than 100 shareholders, or that anticipate having more than 100 shareholders in the future should not consider forming an S corporation due to the limitation on the number of shareholders.

Any business contemplating having shareholders consisting of either partnerships or other corporations. S corporations cannot be owned by partnerships or other corporations.

Any business that has foreign shareholders. All shareholders of an S corporation must be U.S. citizens.

Businesses that would like to accumulate capital within the corporation at lower tax rates. All income is taxed at the shareholders' tax rates which may be higher than the graduated rates of a C corporation, regardless of whether or not cash is distributed.

Businesses that cannot afford the additional cost of incorporating the business, proper accounting, and the additional costs of maintaining the corporate documents.

Businesses that wish to allocate profit and losses in a manner other than on a pro-rata basis. S corporation profit and loss must be proportionately allocated in the same percentage as stock ownership.

Limited Liability Company

What is a limited liability company? A limited liability company is a hybrid entity. A formal entity, organized and registered with the Secretary of State, an LLC has the limited liability protection provided by a corporation and is generally taxed like a partnership or sole proprietor/individual investor, by default.

Ownership. A limited liability company can be owned by one or more persons. There is no limit on the number of persons that can be owners of a limited liability company.

If only one person owns the business, it is known as a single member LLC. If there is more than one owner is it known as a multiple member LLC.

An LLC can be member-managed, or managed by a manager.

Ease of formation. The LLC must register "Articles of Organization" with the Secretary of State. Other than tax reporting, there are no further documents that need to be maintained, unlike the requirements for a corporation.

It is generally a good idea to register your business name with your local authority to ensure no one else is using the name and to reserve your right to use the selected name.

It is also suggested that a formal LLC operating agreement be adopted and signed by all of the LLC members.

Items that should be included:

- Listing of duties and responsibilities of the members
- How the management of the LLC will be handled
- How changes to the LLC ownership will be handled upon the death, disability, retirement or withdrawal of a member
- Requirements for the admission of new members
- How income/losses will be allocated
- How and when member distributions will be made and how they will be determined

- What the capital contributions of the member will be and how the member interests will be divided

LLCs are a formal legally recognized entity. A limited liability company is a formal legal entity whose status is granted by the state in which it is organized.

Legal liability

The members of a limited liability company enjoy limited liability protection from the debts and other obligations of the business. This is generally considered to be one of the main advantages in the forming of an LLC.

It is suggested that an LLC maintain a business checking account, separate and distinct from the personal checking accounts of the members.

Tax reporting

LLCs are unique in that they can elect their tax treatment and even change how they are taxed as their businesses evolve.

The default treatment of a single member LLC is to be taxed like a sole proprietor. All business activity is reported on Schedule E, "Supplemental Income and Loss" of the LLC member's personal tax return.

The default treatment of a multiple member LLC is to be treated like a general partnership. All business activity is reported on Form 1065, "U. S. Return of Partnership Income."

If however, the LLC member(s) decide that the default treatment does not meet their needs, they can make an Entity Classification Election using Form 8832, and select the taxation structure that meets their needs.

The LLC may choose to be taxed as a C corporation or an S corporation. If it elects to be taxed as a particular entity, it must report their activities on the corresponding form. C corporations must use a Form 1120, "U.S. Corporation Income Tax Return." S corporations must use a Form 1120S, "U.S. Income Tax Return for an S Corporation."

Careful consideration must be made before making an election. While an entity election may be changed, that change is irreversible for five years.

How is income allocated?
How income is allocated depends upon the number of members and any elections made.

For a single member LLC, all of the income belongs to the single member.

For a multiple member LLC, net income is allocated by default on a pro-rata basis among the members.

However, a limited liability company, absent an entity election is flexible in how income can be allocated to the members. Income and losses are not required to be allocated based upon the percentage ownership of the members and can be allocated to members in any manner in which they agree.

For example, all of the losses can be allocated to one member and all of the profits can be allocated to another member. Or an allocation can be made on a 75/25 % basis, when, in fact, there are only two members who each own 50%. The only requirement is that the entire amount of income or loss be allocated to someone.

Tax paying
How income is paid depends upon the number of members and any elections made.

For a single member LLC, all of the tax on the LLC income is paid by the single member.

For a multiple member LLC, income is allocated to each individual member, who must report and pay taxes on their pro-rata portion of the income or loss on their personal tax returns.

What taxes are involved?

The member's reported net income is subject to federal income tax. rental income, and is NOT subject to self-employment tax.

For multiple member LLCs, the managing member's income of the business is considered rental income, subject to federal income tax but not subject to self-employment tax.

How are the members paid?

A member can receive two types of income from a limited liability company. Members can receive guaranteed payments to partners for services performed, if those members are actively involved in the business.

Guaranteed payments to members are an expense of the LLC and reduce the net income of the LLC, and therefore the amount of income reported to the members. Guaranteed payments are reported on the appropriate member's Schedule K-1.

Member distributions are usually considered to be a distribution of income, similar to owner draws for a sole proprietor.

Members can have distributions made in any amount deemed appropriate by the members. They do not have to be made in accordance with percentage of ownership.

Member distributions are not considered income to the shareholder and are not subject to self-employment tax.

Member distributions that are made in excess of the balance in their capital account would be reported as income.

Advantages of a Limited Liability Company

Limited liability—LLCs generally have the same limited liability protection as corporations. The liability of members is limited to their investment in the LLC, plus any debts personally guaranteed.

Relatively easy to set up—A limited liability company must file Articles of Organization with the Secretary of State. No other formal organization or legal paperwork is required, such as holding annual shareholder meetings or keeping of corporate minutes, as is required with corporations.

A newly formed limited liability company must obtain an Employer Identification Number (EIN) by completing Form SS-4, "Application for Employer Identification Number." This identifying number will be used by the LLC in all of its tax filings.

Flexibility in how the entity will be taxed—An LLC can change how it chooses to be taxed, as its needs change, by completing a Form 8832, "Entity Classification Election." This can only be done once every five years.

Multiple owners—A limited liability company may have one or more members (owners). An LLC operating with a single member would generally be taxed as a sole proprietor. An LLC with multiple members is generally taxed as a partnership.

There can be an unlimited number of partners in a limited liability company, unless a multiple member LLC chooses to be taxed as an S corporation.

Easier to raise capital—Allowing multiple members to contribute capital to the business and having the ability to borrow money on behalf of the business, and not relying on a single or small number of members' personal credit, increases the capital raising ability of the entity.

More depth of management—Having more than one owner diversifies the management available to the business. The more members involved, the more talent, experience, and skill-sets are available to help grow and run the business.

Simplified payroll—There is no requirement to set up the members as employees and write payroll checks, or handle other responsibilities of having employees such as quarterly payroll tax filings, paying employment taxes and preparing an annual W-2.

If the LLC hires employees, then the entity must comply with all recordkeeping and filing requirements for their employees.

"Pass-through" of losses—Losses "pass through" to the member's personal tax return. These losses can be used to offset other taxable income of the members, subject to certain limitations. This can be important if the LLC generates losses at the beginning of the business.

Deductibility of health insurance premiums—The managing members may deduct up to 100% of health insurance premiums for themselves and their family, limited to the extent of profit reported by the member. Non-managing members are unable to deduct health insurance premiums.

If the member is treated as being self-employed, health insurance premiums do not reduce the LLC's income, but the member can deduct the health insurance premium as an adjustment to income on their personal tax return.

Continuity of life—The death or resignation of a member will not end the life of the LLC. The remaining members can continue operating the business.

No double taxation of profits—All profits flow through to the members who pay tax on their personal tax returns. There is no income tax paid by the LLC such as would be paid by a C corporation, if the LLC has accepted the default tax treatment or if they've elected to be taxed as an S corporation, both of which are "pass-through" treatments (which means there is no "double taxation").

Disadvantages of a Limited Liability Company

More management—Although many people may consider having more partners/members and the additional talent that goes along with more partners as an asset, this may not always be the case.

Human nature will always come into play. Sometimes disagreements will arise concerning business decisions that can be tough to settle.

Complaints about money and draws—There can be major disagreements between the members concerning money. This can be the single largest problem faced by limited liability companies. More LLCs break up over money than any other reason.

Reasons for disagreements can include uneven distributions of profit based upon capital contributed, effort expended or results achieved. For example, two members may put equal time into the business but one may bring in 90% of the sales and the other only 10%. The fellow who brings in 90% of the clients may begin to feel taken advantage of. It's human nature.

A well-drafted LLC agreement should thoroughly address how member distributions should be handled.

Taxed on income—Members are personally responsible for the tax due on their pro-rata profits of the business, regardless of whether profits or money were taken from the business.

However, it is quite common for the LLC to make distributions to the members (which are not considered income) to cover the tax liability incurred by the members as a result of LLC income.

Difficulty raising capital—It can be much tougher raising capital as an LLC. The assets of the members and the LLC serve as the primary collateral for loans, which may not be enough for some lenders.

Who is a Limited Liability Company Best Suited For?

A limited liability company should be considered by real estate investors who wish to limit their exposure to liability.

A limited liability company should be considered by real estate investors with businesses that are just commencing operations. LLCs offer new businesses with much flexibility.

Many new businesses are not profitable in the first year or two and generate losses. Losses generated by the LLC can be used by the members to reduce their taxable income from other sources of income such as a working spouse, rental properties or investment income.

Limited liability companies have flexibility in ownership. An LLC can have as many owners as desired (assuming an S corporation election has not been made).

The only expense of formation is organizing with the Secretary of State. No other formal documentation is required, other than a formal accounting for business and tax purposes.

Who Should Not Operate as a Limited Liability Company

Real estate investors that are not concerned with any potential liability exposure. This is one of the main non-tax features of an LLC. If you don't require limited liability, you can save money on organization costs by not forming an LLC.

Real estate investment businesses with multiple members who are not familiar with one another. It is suggested that you know your member/partner very well before going into business with them. Working closely together is like being married - and you want make sure you know your partner very well before embarking on such a venture.

Ideally, partners/members should bring different sets of skills to the business, such as having one member exceptionally talented in marketing, and another member/partner with complementary skills such as finance or operations.

An age-old saying, "Two heads are better than one" can be very helpful in a small business partnership.

Chapter 16

Not Getting Competent Professional Help

This is probably the most serious mistake of all, and fortunately, the most easily correctable.

Most real estate investors are great at finding and financing deals and running their investment business.

However, the tax side of their real estate investment business, is usually not one of their stronger points.

Tax rules and regulations are very complex and hard to understand. And every year sees many changes to the rules and regulations.

It takes years of training and experience to become a completely competent financial and tax professional. In today's rapidly changing world, it takes 40 to 80 hours per year of advanced training just to keep our skills sharp.

The tax laws related to the real estate investment business are relatively narrow, but are complex, and take years to master!!

Recently, more and more people are falling into the trap of buying $29 tax software and thinking that this will help them know as much as a CPA with years of training and experience.

While tax software is certainly good and getting better all the time, they are simply tools to be used to make the job easier.

They do a great job of putting the right amounts in the right boxes and making sure the mathematical calculations are correct.

However, if you aren't on top of all the constantly changing tax rules and complex tax strategies and how to make them apply to you and your real estate investment business for maximum benefit, the tax software is not going to be of much use to you in your efforts to take advantage of all the legal tax-saving possibilities.

While the software might be good at putting the right information into the right boxes, no software will ever be able to analyze your *personal* tax situation and that of your real estate investment business and suggest the many strategies available to stop paying taxes that you don't have to pay.

To think that you can do-it-yourself, given the many tax complexities in the real estate investment business, doesn't make much sense and will cost you and your business literally thousands of dollars in the long run.

Final Thoughts

I trust the information in this book will be helpful to you.

My goal in sharing it with you is to give you the basic information necessary to help you begin to consider ways in which you can legally reduce the taxes in your real estate investment business.

There are many factors that must be always be evaluated, taking into account your personal situation.

But to begin to reduce your taxes, it is ***up to you*** to take the next step.

I understand that making changes in life can sometimes be uncomfortable, and not something that you may look forward to doing without at least a little apprehension.

However, the sooner you have implemented your personal Strategic Tax Plan™, the sooner you will be able to enjoy the tax savings that will keep more money in your pocket and increase your wealth, rather than in the vaults of the IRS.

Frequently Asked Questions about the Strategic Tax Reduction Process™

Is tax planning legal? Absolutely. Courts have upheld your right to structure your affairs in a manner that *legally* lowers your tax liability.

In many cases, some of the tax laws have been designed specifically with the real estate investor in mind.

Some of these options and strategies can literally save you thousands of tax dollars. And many of these options are unavailable to taxpayers who have a job and are employees of someone else, rather than being a real estate investor.

However, you must take positive, proactive steps to structure your affairs to legally pay the least amount of tax as possible.

What is the difference between tax planning and tax avoidance?
Tax planning is something we have already discussed, and I hope you understand that this is perfectly legal.

Tax evasion, on the other hand, is the reduction of tax through illegal, fraudulent means. What is really involved here is intent. What distinguishes tax planning from tax evasion generally is the intent to commit fraud.

What are some of the main things we do in Strategic Tax Planning?

Strategic Tax Planning is a process that encompasses several different things.

In general, our goal is to reduce taxable income. Taxable income is defined as total income from all sources minus adjustments to income, minus itemized deductions, and minus personal exemptions.

If we reduce taxable income, then by definition and by law we will be reducing the Federal Income Tax.

The first way in which we do this is to receive income and/or benefits that are not taxable income.

Second, we try to make sure and capture all of the deductions to which we are entitled. This of course begins with having a proper accounting system to capture all of the expenses and the deductions of the business.

Other strategies we concentrate on is how to take advantage of the best retirement plan for our situation and shifting income to other family members.

What is the most important step in tax planning? The first and most important step involved in tax planning would be the selection of the proper entity in which to operate your business.

Selecting the form of business entity you choose to operate your real estate investment business is the single biggest decision you will make. It will have a direct impact on how you operate your business, what benefits you will personally receive, and how much you will pay in tax.

Because the first thing we must evaluate during a tax planning engagement is selecting the best business entity, I authored a book, ***The Official Business Owner's Guide to Selecting a Business Entity: How Every New and Existing Business Can Choose the Best Entity to Operate Their Business.***

Remember, selecting your business entity is going to determine how you are going to be taxed, the taxes involved, and what deductible benefits and retirement benefits you may be entitled to.

How likely is it that I will save tax dollars if I do tax planning?

There is actually a very good chance that you can save money by going through a Strategic Tax Planning engagement.

There are only two instances I am aware of in which you wouldn't be able to save taxes by doing a Strategic Tax Planning engagement.

The first of these is the situation in which a real estate investor is making very little money and hence paying little in taxes. It would be difficult to implement any tax planning strategies in this situation, as there is not much tax liability to begin with.

The second instance would be a situation where a real estate investor has already implemented all of the strategies that would be appropriate in their situation.

In practice, I haven't really seen this happen. There seems to always be at least one or more strategies to implement to reduce your taxes.

What does the term "proactive" tax planning mean?

The dictionary defines proactive as *"serving to prepare for, intervene in, or control an expected occurrence or situation, especially a negative or difficult one."*

Proactive, as it relates to tax planning, simply means you do the tax planning ***in advance***....as this gives us as many of the available options as possible. The opposite of proactive, in the tax planning world, would be doing little to no planning in advance.

There may still be decisions to make and things to do after the fact...such as when someone comes to see me after the end of the tax year...but at that point, not all of the options are available to us, and therefore, money we could have saved will have been lost.

We have to wait for the following year to implement many of the strategies, and realize the tax savings in a later year.

Why should I do tax planning now rather than next year or later?

In the financial world, it is always better to save a dollar today than a dollar tomorrow. And typically with tax planning, not only will you save money today, you will also save money in the future. So it just makes sense to start saving money today rather than tomorrow.

Will I have to change the way that I am doing business?

Maybe, maybe not...Like many things related to tax, it just depends. The

Are you already structured in the form of business entity that is best for your business – one that will allow you to implement the best strategies for reducing your taxes? Other than the form of business entity, you will generally continue to do things in your business the same as you are doing them now.

How much tax savings can I expect to realize by doing proactive Strategic Tax Planning?

While of course every investor has a different situation, most investor can enjoy a tax savings of at least two to three thousand dollars a year. Many times the savings can be $5,000 or even more. It just depends on your particular situation. I recently completed tax planning engagements that yielded $6,384 in savings for one client, and another that will yield $9,595. And that is *per year* savings!!! So you can see, when you multiply these tax savings by a number of years in the future, we are talking about serious amounts of money.

What can I expect at my initial meeting?

The initial meeting is really just an information gathering meeting. I will need to find out about your current situation and I will do that by asking you a series of questions and reviewing your most recent personal and business tax returns.

I will ask you about what some of your goals are, and a bit about your family. I will be evaluating your initial situation to determine if I think that there is a possibility that you are a good candidate for a Strategic Tax Reduction engagement and whether I think we will be successful in realizing any tax savings. I will offer you a ballpark estimate of what I think your tax savings will be, and what the fee involved to proceed and prepare a detailed comprehensive Tax Plan would be.

The Types of Clients That I Accept

I am very selective about the kinds of clients that I accept into my practice.

The first criteria I am looking for in an individual is someone who owns either a new or existing real estate investment business. Many but not all of the tax strategies that I suggest and employ are only available to real estate investors.

The investor must be the main decision maker. If an investor has no ability to make the final decision to implement a particular strategy, all the tax planning strategies that I suggest will be useless. Implementation is critical.

An investor must be open to new ideas and willing to change. If a investor doesn't want to change anything in the way they structure their affairs, nothing will change in their situation and the taxes that they pay.

The investor must be honest and ethical and willing to work within the rules and regulations of the IRS. Clients interested in intentionally understating income or overstating expenses are committing fraud, and I will not knowingly become involved with these types of taxpayers.

If any of these situations describes you, please feel free to call. My practice is set up to help you realize the most savings possible on your taxes!

The Types of Clients That I Don't Accept

I enjoy working with investors to help them minimize their taxes through Strategic Tax Planning.

If an investor wants to continue doing things the way they have always done them, and is not open to change, they will not benefit from a Strategic Tax Planning engagement with me.

By definition, unless an investor has already structured their affairs to minimize their taxes, the Strategic Tax Plan will suggest a different way of doing things from the way that things have been done in the past.

Clients who are interested in filing fraudulent tax returns don't need tax planning and are not people I will work with. The IRS statute of limitations for FRAUD is unlimited – the IRS has forever to audit any returns that they suspect are fraudulent. And, "forever" is a very long time.

So if any of these situations describes you, please don't call. My practice is not set up to help you!

About the Author

Larry M. Weinstein is a CPA, a Certified Tax Reduction Strategist® and the Managing Director of TaxSavingsForRealEstateInvestors.com.

Larry graduated from the University of Houston with a BBA in Accounting, and began his career in the Houston office of the world-renowned accounting firm Arthur Young, now known as Ernst & Young.

In private practice since 1988, Larry concentrates in the area of Strategic Tax Planning and Preparation, mostly for Real Estate Investors, closely held businesses, and the owners of these businesses.

For over 30 years, Larry has been a Tax Advisor to the real estate industry.

During his career, he has represented, counseled, and done high level strategic tax planning and preparation for scores of real estate clients ranging from brand new investors to a multi-millionaire real estate investor with over 25 apartment complexes, and everything in between.

Larry is also an active real estate investor. His over 30 years of experience suggests that most real estate investors are overpaying their taxes and, most likely, you are overpaying your taxes as well!!

Larry is the developer of the Strategic Real Estate Tax Reduction Process ™ and lives in Houston, Texas with his wife and daughters.

Glossary of Terms

Accelerated Depreciation a method of recording depreciation faster than with straight line depreciation. More depreciation is recorded in the earlier years than in the later years.

Accrual Basis the method of accounting that looks at whether income has been earned (whether or not received), and whether an expense has been incurred (whether or not paid).

Buy-Sell Agreement an agreement detailing the future buyout of partners or owners.

C Corporation a corporation that chooses to be taxed at the corporate level.

Capital an account that tracks an owner's or partner's interest in the business.

Cash Basis the method of accounting that records income when actually received, and expenses when actually paid.

DBA "doing business as" – the registering of your business name with the local city or state authorities. Also known as a *fictitious name.*

Double Taxation describes the situation where an entity pays tax once at the corporate level, and the income is taxed a second time when it is paid to the taxpayer.

Estimated Tax Payment a quarterly tax payment made during the year for estimated annual tax liability.

Effective Tax Rate total tax paid divided by total income.

Form 1040 the form used to file an individual's personal tax return.

Form 1065 the form used to file a partnership tax return.

Form 1120 the form used to file a C corporation tax return.

Form 1120S the form used to file an S corporation tax return.

Form 2553 the election form used to request S corporation status.

Form 8823 the election form used to select the desired method of taxation when forming an LLC.

General Partner an owner of a general partnership, or the managing partner in a limited partnership.

General Partnership an unincorporated business operated by two or more individuals.

Limited Liability Company an entity owned by one or more owners in which the owners have limited liability.

Limited Partnership a partnership in which the limited partners have limited liability. One or more general partners have unlimited liabilities.

Marginal Tax Rate the tax rate that applies to the next dollar a taxpayer earns.

Member an owner of a limited liability company (LLC).

Multiple member LLC an LLC that has more than one owner/member.

Partner an owner of a partnership.

Pass-through entity an entity that reports their taxes, but doesn't pay their taxes. Income or loss is "passed through" to the owners of the business who pay the tax.

Owner Draw profit distribution taken by a sole proprietorship from their business.

Partnership distribution money paid from a partnership to a partner.

S Corporation Distribution money paid from an S corporation to a shareholder.

Schedule C form used to report income and expenses of a sole proprietorship.

Self employment tax tax paid on the earnings of a self-employed individual. Similar to the Social Security and Medicare tax.

Shareholder an owner of a corporation.

Single Member LLC a limited liability company with only one member/owner, as opposed to multiple member/owners. Treated as a sole proprietor for tax purposes.

Sole Proprietorship an unincorporated business operated by a single individual.

Tax Credit an item on a personal tax returns that reduces the tax owed dollar for dollar ($1 dollar tax credit equals $1 dollar of tax savings).

Tax Deduction an expense item on the tax return that reduces taxable income dollar for dollar. Tax reductions reduce tax by the amount of the marginal tax bracket.

Tax Savings a reduction in tax that would otherwise have been paid before tax planning.

Taxable Income the net income amount subject to federal income tax. Represents total income less adjustments less itemized or standard deduction and less personal exemptions.

Made in United States
[illegible] CT
[illegible]

Made in United States
North Haven, CT
04 November 2026

21763943R00075